Build Your Own WEB SITE

By Laura Buller

CELEBRATION PRESS
Pearson Learning Group

The following people from **Pearson Learning Group**
have contributed to the development of this product:

Dorothea Fox, Joan Mazzeo **Design** | **Editorial** Leslie Feierstone-Barna, Teri Crawford-Jones
Christine Fleming **Marketing** | **Publishing Operations** Jennifer Van Der Heide
Production Laura Benford-Sullivan
Content Area Consultant Amy Keller

The following people from **DK** have
contributed to the development of this product:

Art Director Rachael Foster
Martin Wilson **Managing Art Editor** | **Managing Editor** Marie Greenwood
Spencer Holbrook **Design** | **Editorial** Selina Wood
Brenda Clynch **Picture Research** | **Production** Gordana Simakovic
Richard Czapnik, Andy Smith **Cover Design** | **DTP** David McDonald
Consultant Tim Ryan

Dorling Kindersley would like to thank: Clair Watson for additional design work; Peter Bull for illustration; Andy Crawford for photography;
Lucy Heaver for editorial assistance; Emily McHugh and Neel Shah for modelling; Rose Horridge in the DK Picture Library;
Johnny Pau for additional cover design work.

Screen shots reprinted by permission from Microsoft Corporation. DK would also like to thank Ask Jeeves, Inc., Apple Computer, Inc., and
The Natural History Museum, London, for use of additional screen shots.

Picture Credits: Jim Cummins 30bc, 31bc, 32bc, 33cr, 34bc, 36bc, 37cr; Michael Kevin Daly 8cra; Raymond Gehman 8cr; Onne van der Wal 8crb.

All other images: ˮ Dorling Kindersley © 2005. For further information see www.dkimages.com

For information regarding licensing and permissions, write to Rights and Permissions Department, Pearson Learning Group,
299 Jefferson Road, Parsippany, NJ 07054 USA or to Rights and Permissions Department, DK Publishing,
The Penguin Group (UK), 80 Strand, London WC2R 0RL.

ISBN: 0-7652-5257-0

Color reproduction by Colourscan, Singapore
Printed in the United States of America
4 5 6 7 8 9 10   08

1-800-321-3106
www.pearsonlearning.com

Contents

What You Need to Know

The **Internet** has changed the way that many of us search for information. We can visit countless sites on the **World Wide Web** to find information about almost anything when we use a computer.

If you have ever visited a Web site, written an e-mail, or typed a report on a computer, you'll find this book's step-by-step instructions for creating your own Web site easy to follow. Even if you don't have much computer experience, you can still build a Web site. The glossary will help you understand many important terms. The list of Web sites on page 39 tells you where you can go for additional tips.

Byte Box

Look for "byte boxes" throughout the book to learn more about the World Wide Web and its history.

Meet Browzer, the wonder dog of the Web. Browzer will appear from time to time to offer helpful tips.

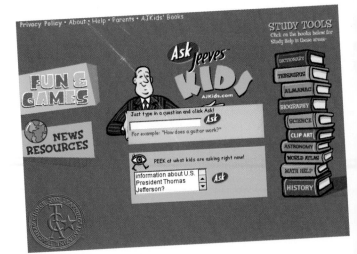

This Web site (www.ajkids.com) helps you find what you are searching for by providing a list of Web sites that are related to your keyword, phrase or question.

A Word of Caution

The Internet is an exciting place. Like many exciting places, though, it has some risks. If you create a Web site and put it on the Internet, strangers—as well as friends and family—will be able to see it. So, it's very important not to put personal information on your Web site.

Be Safe!

Here are some guidelines for your Web creations.
- Never put your (or anyone else's) last name, address, photograph, or telephone number on a Web site.
- Never put information on a Web site that a stranger could use to identify who you are or where you live.
- Always remember that the Internet is a public place. Never put anything there that you wouldn't want the whole world to see. Use courteous and respectful language and images.
- Always have a parent or guardian check your Web page before you put it on the Internet.

Web Basics

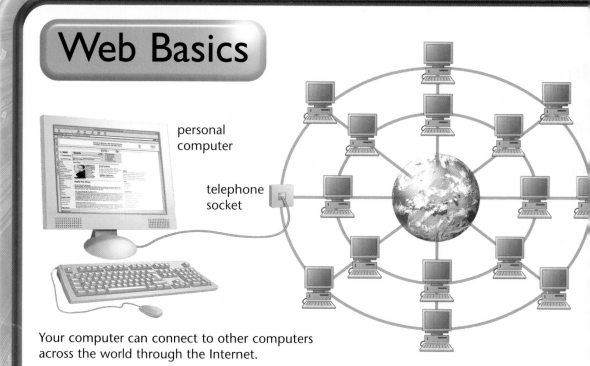

personal computer

telephone socket

Your computer can connect to other computers across the world through the Internet.

The Internet is a huge **network** of connected computers. The computers are connected through modems, direct wires, telephone lines, and wireless connections. Until your computer is connected into this network, you are not on the Internet.

The Web is part of the Internet. It allows different types of computer files, such as text, pictures, sound, and video to be accessed around the world. When these files reach your computer, the computer software—the programs or files that allow the computer to operate—translates them into pictures and text that appear on the computer screen.

Byte Box

The Web was the idea of an English scientist, Timothy Berners-Lee. He invented **HTML**, the text based programming language used to build Web sites.

Internet Browsers

The computer's **browser** enables you to move around the Web. A browser is software on your computer that takes the files from the Web and converts them into Web pages so you can view and read them. Netscape Navigator®, Microsoft Internet Explorer®, and Apple Safari® are the names of three common browsers. The browser reads a special code in the files that tells it how to show the pages. The most common code system is HTML (short for *hypertext markup language*). This means that the codes are written in a text-based language, such as English, not in a number-based language. To create your Web site, you will learn some basic HTML code.

Viewing HTML Code

At this site, http://www.dk.com, you can find out more about the company that published this book. To see the HTML code used to create the Web page shown, click on the *View* menu at the top left of your browser. Then select *Source* or *Page Source* from the drop-down menu. A window will display the HTML code. It may look like nonsense, but you'll soon learn how it works.

HTML code

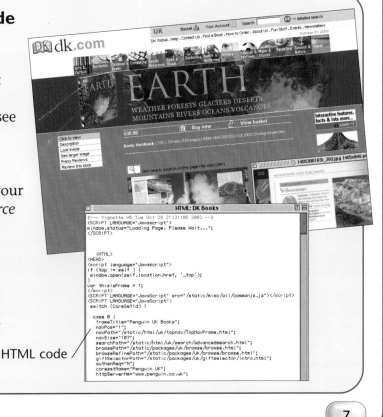

Planning a Web Site

It's worth spending some time preparing for the development of your Web site. This will save you time and trouble later on. Think about what you want your Web site to be about, how you want it to look, and who will read it. Jot down some ideas in a notepad.

What will your Web site be about?

- Favorite sports, such as soccer or basketball
- A school club that you and your friends belong to
- An interest, such as space or nature
- A school trip or a vacation

Remember that Web sites can be read by anyone who has access to the Internet.

What will it look like?

Take a look at other Web sites to gain ideas about how you would like your Web site to look. Think about:

- Colors
- Font type and size
- Images you would like

Structuring your Web site

How large do you want your site to be? How are you going to present the information? Will it have more than one page?

Sketch how you want your Web site to look on paper first...

...then map out how many pages you want and where they are linked to one another.

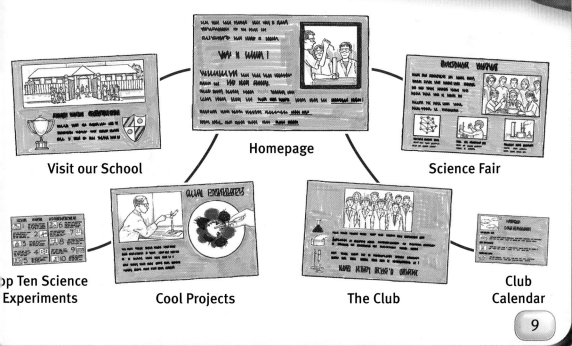

Visit our School

Homepage

Science Fair

op Ten Science Experiments

Cool Projects

The Club

Club Calendar

Code Basics

The HTML code is written in a simple text file that uses the same letters, numbers, and other characters that you use to type an e-mail or a report. You type the words that you want to appear on your Web page into the HTML file, along with instructions about where the words should go and how big the type font should be. If the site has images, the HTML code tells the browser where to find those image files and how to display them. HTML directs these browser actions through the use of special signals called **tags**.

Creating a Web site is almost as easy as typing a letter.

A Game of Tag

Most tags use abbreviations (for example, "b" for bold type).

Tags are letters, words, or symbols that tell the browser program what to show on a Web page. All tags begin with a left bracket (<). This indicates that the next letters are an instruction. Then comes the instruction itself, a series of symbols for tasks. Finally, the tag ends with a right bracket (>).

For example, let's imagine that the subject of your Web site is your school science club, The Lab Rats.

You want the name of the club to appear in bold text to make it really stand out. The tag for bold text looks like this: <b>.

The tag is inserted right before the word "The" in the club's name.

<b>The Lab Rats

Your browser will see the <b> tag, follow the command, and produce this:

The Lab Rats

Each tag represents a different task. There's a tag to make the text bigger, a tag to change the text color, and a tag to center the text on the page. Usually, you place a tag right in front of a word to tell your browser that it has a job to do.

11

Ending a Tag

Your browser will follow your command. For example, it will make everything bold text until you tell it to stop. You will need to insert another tag (sometimes called a closing tag) to tell the browser to stop the bold. A closing tag looks like an opening tag but includes a backslash (/). The tag to end bold text looks like this: </b>.

So, to see your club's name appear in bold text, you use the following:

<b>The Lab Rats</b>

Remember, you're in command. The browser only does what you tell it to do. Be sure to type accurately. If you don't put the tag in properly, the browser will ignore it. When something you are trying to do on your Web page doesn't work, a typing error is most likely the source of the problem.

Remember to type carefully! The browser does exactly what you tell it to.

File Basics

HTML files are created with programs called text editors. Text editors that are good for writing HTML are Notepad if you use a Window® PC (Personal Computer) and TextEdit or SimpleText if you use an Apple Macintosh®. (Not all text editors work with HTML, and some will add codes you can't see. So, it's best to use Notepad and TextEdit to begin with.)

When you open your text editor file, you may want to size the window on your computer screen so that you can move easily back and forth between it and your browser. If you like, you can make a window disappear when you're not using it by clicking on the minimize box or circle in the upper right-hand corner. Clicking on the box again or on the name at the bottom of the screen will make the window reappear or reopen.

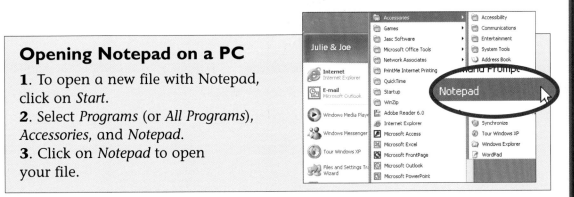

Opening Notepad on a PC

1. To open a new file with Notepad, click on *Start*.
2. Select *Programs* (or *All Programs*), *Accessories*, and *Notepad*.
3. Click on *Notepad* to open your file.

Opening TextEdit on an Apple Mac

1. To open a new file with TextEdit, double-click on *Macintosh HD* (hard drive) from the desktop.
2. Double-click on the *Applications* folder.
3. Double-click on *TextEdit* to open a file.

Web Page Beginnings

To begin a Web page you need these basic tags: <html>, <head>, and <title>. The <html> tag shows your browser where the files for the Web page begin. So, always start an HTML file by typing this: <html>.

At the end of the document, to show your browser where the Web page files end, use this tag: </html>.

The <head> tag begins the heading. The heading on a Web page doesn't show up on the screen. Headings can contain information about the page, such as the name of the page. They also can contain the key words for listing your page in **search engines** and headings can also contain a page title.

```
<html>
<head>
<title>Meet The Lab Rats</title>
</head>
```

The title, as typed above, doesn't show on the Web page. It appears on the browser's title bar at the top of the screen.

Note that the <html> tag begins the document.

The <head> tag opens the heading.

Next, the <title> tag opens "Meet The Lab Rats," and then the </title> tag closes it.

Untitled - Notepad

File   Edit   Format   View   Help

```
<html>
<head>
<title>Meet The Lab Rats</title>
</head>
```

Then the </head> tag closes the heading. Your browser won't read the file as being complete or finished, however, because the </html> tag isn't here.

Beginning Your Web Page

To make a Web page, you will need a computer with a text editor and a browser.

When you type your HTML text, you may want to press the return key, called a hard return, to make the text easy to read. These breaks will not show on your Web page.

Type the Heading

1. Open a new file in your text editor. Type in these lines:

```
<html>
<head>
<title>Meet The Lab Rats</title>
</head>
</html>
```

2. Check your work. Even a tiny typing mistake could cause the instruction to fail. Type all characters, words, and spaces exactly as shown.

Untitled - Notepad

File   Edit   Format   View   Help

```
<html>
<head>
<title>Meet The Lab Rats</title
</head>
```

Check for any typing errors

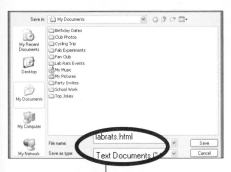

Save your file as labrats.html

3. Save the file as *labrats.html* so the computer and browser will know how to handle the file, but don't close the file or exit your text editor yet. Be sure to save the file in a place where you can find it again. One of the best locations to save your files is in a folder on the hard drive.

Type the Main Text

So far we've made the Web file's heading. It won't show on the actual Web page (except in the title bar).

1. We now need to add a new tag. The <body> tag allows you to type in the actual text that will show up on the page. Add the following lines to your file. Your text editor file is still open.

> <body>Welcome to our weird and wonderful science club: The Lab Rats! Meet the Rats, check out our cool science projects, find out more about our club, visit our school, and see how we did in the Science Fair!</body>
> </html>

We closed the body with the </body> tag and ended the file with the </html> tag.

2. Resave the file. You have now made a Web page. Let's look at it. There's no need to close this page.

> Your computer doesn't mind if you use upper or lowercase letters in the tags. Some people think that uppercase letters are easier to find if you need to go back and fix anything.

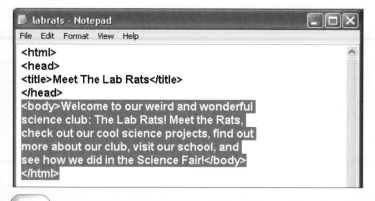

```
labrats - Notepad
File  Edit  Format  View  Help
<html>
<head>
<title>Meet The Lab Rats</title>
</head>
<body>Welcome to our weird and wonderful
science club: The Lab Rats! Meet the Rats,
check out our cool science projects, find out
more about our club, visit our school, and
see how we did in the Science Fair!</body>
</html>
```

Displaying Your Web Page

Let's see how your Web page looks by opening it up on the browser.

Open Your Browser

1. If you use a Windows PC, you may have a shortcut to the browser (see p. 7). This may be on the desktop or the *Start* taskbar. Then you can open your browser with a single click.

2. On a Windows PC you may need to click *Start*, select *Programs*, then click on the browser name. On a Macintosh you may find the browser in the Apple Menu under *Recent Applications*.

3. You may also find an icon for the browser on the desktop or the icon and a name on the hard drive. Click on the icon or the name in order to open the browser.

Were you successful in opening your browser? The exact steps used vary. They depend upon the type of computer, operating system, and browser you are using.

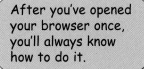

After you've opened your browser once, you'll always know how to do it.

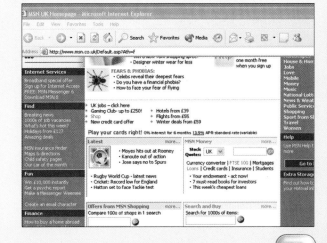

Find the File

When the browser is running, tell it where to look for your HTML file—which will be in the folder where you saved it.

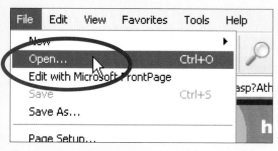

1. Select *File* from the browser's menu bar. From the drop-down menu, choose *Open*. (If you're using a Macintosh select *Open File* or *Open Page* and go directly to step 3.)

2. The browser opens a dialogue box, choose *Browse* or *Choose File* to look for your file.

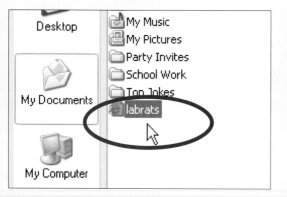

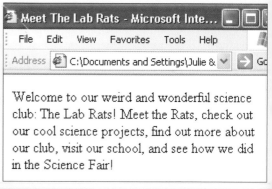

3. A window opens that shows a list of files and folders. Find the file named *labrats* and double-click, or click once and select *Open* or *OK*. (Your computer may display your file as *labrats.html*.)

4. Your web page should now appear.

Check Your Results

If your words don't appear on the browser, it's likely that you've made a typing mistake. Leave your browser window open as you go back to the *labrats* file, and check your work very carefully.

Write your HTML code in either uppercase or lowercase letters. It's best to use only one case.

```
labrats - Notepad
File  Edit  Format  View  Help
<html>
<head>
<title>Meet The Lab Rats</title>
</head>
<body>Welcome to our weird and wonderful
science club: The Lab Rats! Meet the Rats,
check out our cool science projects, find out
more about our club, visit our school, and
see how we did in the Science Fair!</body>
</html>
```

1. Make sure brackets are correct.

2. Check that all the backslashes (/) are facing the correct way.

3. Check that the spacing is the same as in the sample.

4. Check that you've opened and closed all tags.

5. When you finish making changes, save the file again.

6. Return to the browser (by clicking its window or bar) and click on *View* on the menu bar, then click on *Refresh* or *Reload*. Any changes you made in the file now appear.

Address C:\Documents and Settings\Julie & Go

Welcome to our weird and wonderful science club: The Lab Rats! Meet the Rats, check out our cool science projects, find out more about our club, visit our school, and see how we did in the Science Fair!

Inserting Text Tags

So far your page is plain text. Using the tags in this section will help you create a site that is easy to read.

Paragraphs and Breaks

The paragraph tag tells the browser to skip a line, and then start a new paragraph. (Paragraphs are separated by a line space. Their first lines will not be indented.) The paragraph tag looks like this: <p>

If you want to move to the next line without skipping a line space, use a break tag. A break tag works like the return key on your keyboard. It looks like this:

These two tags do not require a closing tag.

1. Return to Notepad without closing your Web page. Add a break to your body text. The <br> tag should be placed right where you want the line to turn. Add the following tag to your file, typing carefully.

```
<body>Welcome to our weird
and wonderful science
club: The Lab Rats!
<br>
Meet the Rats, check out our
cool science projects, find out
more about our club, visit our
school, and see how we did in
the Science Fair!</body>
</html>
```

labrats - Notepad

File   Edit   Format   View   Help

```
<html>
<head>
<title>Meet The Lab Rats</title>
</head>
<body>Welcome to our weird and
wonderful science club: The Lab Rats!
<br>
Meet the Rats, check out our cool
science projects, find out more about
our club, visit our school, and see how
we did in the Science Fair!</body>
</html>
```

2. Resave the file. Go to the Web page and hit *Refresh* or *Reload*. You should see your break.

Remember, you format from the outside in. The major instruction—telling the computer that the file is HTML—is farthest outside. A specific instruction about the format of words, such as telling the computer to underline a word, is placed before the word.

Meet The Lab Rats - Microsoft Inter...

File   Edit   View   Favorites   Tools   Help

Address   C:\Documents and Settings\Julie & J   Go

Welcome to our weird and wonderful science club: The Lab Rats!
Meet the Rats, check out our cool science projects, find out more about our club, visit our school, and see how we did in the Science Fair!

Text Styles

To make words or phrases stand out, you can make them **bold**, *italic*, or <u>underline</u> them. The codes for these styles all require an opening and closing tag. You already know how to use the tags for **bold** text (see page 11). If you want text to appear in *italics*, use this tag: <i>. If you want the text to be <u>underlined</u>, use this tag: <u>.

1. Add some bold words to your body text. Add the <b> tag right before the first word you want in bold and the closing tag </b> after the last word. Your screen should look like the one on the right.

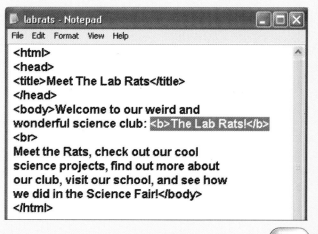

labrats - Notepad

File   Edit   Format   View   Help

```
<html>
<head>
<title>Meet The Lab Rats</title>
</head>
<body>Welcome to our weird and
wonderful science club: <b>The Lab Rats!</b>
<br>
Meet the Rats, check out our cool
science projects, find out more about
our club, visit our school, and see how
we did in the Science Fair!</body>
</html>
```

You can adjust the size of the type by using the **font** tag. There are seven font (type) sizes, numbered from 1 (the smallest) to 7 (the largest). Put the number in your tag where the "#" is in the sample. For example: <font size=#>your text</font>. Font size 3 is called the default size. A default is a value (or size, in this case) that the computer will display if you don't specify anything.

2. Change the size of the word *Welcome* in your text. Add the tag as shown.

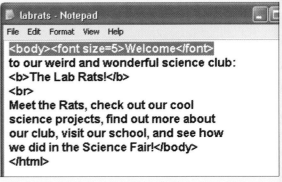

You can also decide which font to use. The default font is Times New Roman. Arial, Helvetica, and Comic Sans MS are examples of other font names. You can include the font name and size instructions in the same tag.

3. Change the font of the word *Welcome* on your page. Add the instruction to the font tag as shown.

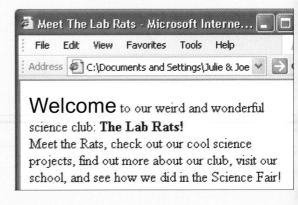

```
<font face=Arial size=5>
Welcome</font>
```

Note that the closing tag </font> closes the font instruction. The text then changes back to the default font type and size.

Headlines and Alignment

Headlines organize the text on your page. Headlines come in different sizes, just as fonts do. They range from <h1> to <h6>, with <h1> being the largest. The headline code has an opening and closing tag.

1. Add the headline "What a Club!" to the beginning of your body text by typing the copy shown on the screen below.

```
labrats - Notepad
File  Edit  Format  View  Help

<body><h2>What a Club!</h2>
<font face=Arial size=5>Welcome</font>
to our weird and wonderful science club:
<b>The Lab Rats!</b>
<br>
Meet the Rats, check out our cool
science projects, find out more about
our club, visit our school, and see how
we did in the Science Fair!</body>
</html>
```

Do you want your text to line up against the left side of the page, float in the center, or stay to the right? The <p> tag **aligns** text to the left automatically. To center a paragraph, use this tag: <p align=center>. To align a paragraph to the right, use this tag: <p align=right>. Remember, all the text that follows these instructions will align in the same way—unless you give a new instruction.

2. Try centering the headline you just added to your Web page. Add the copy shown on the screen to your headline tag.

```
labrats - Notepad
File  Edit  Format  View  Help
<body><h2 align=center>What a Club!</h2>
<font face=Arial size=5>Welcome</font>
to our weird and wonderful science club:
<b>The Lab Rats!</b>
<br>
Meet the Rats, check out our cool
science projects, find out more about
our club, visit our school, and see how
we did in the Science Fair!</body>
</html>
```

Meet The Lab Rats - Microsoft Internet ...
File Edit View Favorites Tools Help
Address C:\Documents and Settings\Julie & Joe\M

What a Club!

Welcome to our weird and wonderful
science club: **The Lab Rats!**
Meet the Rats, check out our cool science
projects, find out more about our club, visit our
school, and see how we did in the Science Fair!

Text Links

You can easily link your site with another site on the Web. Then visitors can click on a word or series of words that will take them to the linked site. The tags for links are called anchor tags and look like this:

```
<a href=www.webaddress></a>
```

In the code, replace "www.webaddress" with the correct **URL**, or Web site address, of a linked site. The "a" of the code stands for "anchor." The "href" stands for "hypertext reference," which refers to the address of the site you are linking to. The anchor tag must be both opened and closed, and the space between "a" and "href" *must* be present. To make a link, decide which words on the Web page become the "hot spot"—the place where visitors click to go to the linked page. Put the hot spot word or phrase between the anchor tags, and include the Web address inside the first tag. When the hot spot shows up on the browser, the link is usually blue and underlined.

1. Try adding a link to your text. Use the words "visit our school" in the Lab Rats' site to link it to your school's Web site. First, return to your HTML file.

2. Add the link text and tags as shown.

```
labrats - Notepad
File  Edit  Format  View  Help

<body><h2 align=center>What a Club!</h2>
<font face=Arial size=5>Welcome</font>
to our weird and wonderful science club:
<b>The Lab Rats!</b>
<br>
Meet the Rats, check out our cool
science projects, find out more about our club,
<a href=http://www.yourschoolwebaddress>
visit our school</a>, and see how
we did in the Science Fair!</body>
</html>
```

Notice that there are no spaces between any of the characters, from *href* to the closing tag. Remember to close off a link with the </a> tag, or your whole page will become one long link!

3. Save your file.

4. Open, reload, or refresh your browser. Your screen should look like the one below.

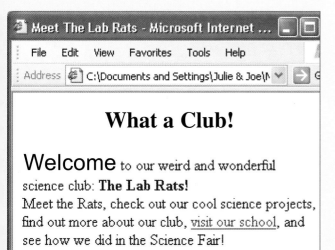

Meet The Lab Rats - Microsoft Internet ...
File Edit View Favorites Tools Help
Address C:\Documents and Settings\Julie & Joe\M

What a Club!

Welcome to our weird and wonderful science club: **The Lab Rats!**
Meet the Rats, check out our cool science projects, find out more about our club, visit our school, and see how we did in the Science Fair!

Using Color

Choose colors carefully. You might think hot pink text on a lime green background looks great, but if it makes text hard to read, choose something else. Be aware that blue text for linked sites may not show up on some backgrounds.

Now, it's time to learn how to bring color to your site. You can color the background, the text, or both!

Add Color to Your Page

If you want to add a splash of color to your entire page, name the color in the <body> tag at the beginning of your HTML document. For example: <body bgcolor=?>. When you use this tag, you replace "?" with the name of a color.

1. Try making the Lab Rats' site more attractive by using some color. Add yellow as the background color. Type in the body text tag as shown.

2. Check your result.

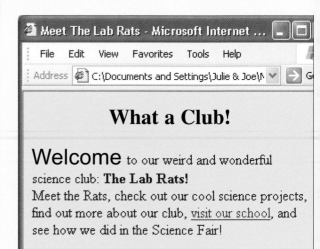

```
labrats - Notepad
File  Edit  Format  View  Help

<body bgcolor=yellow>
<h2 align=center>What a Club!</h2>
<font face=Arial size=5>Welcome
</font> to our weird and wonderful
science club:
<b>The Lab Rats!</b>
<br>
Meet the Rats, check out our cool
science projects, find out more about
our club, <a href=http://www.your
schoolwebaddress>
visit our school</a>, and see how
we did in the Science Fair!</body>
</html>
```

Meet The Lab Rats - Microsoft Internet ...
File Edit View Favorites Tools Help
Address C:\Documents and Settings\Julie & Joe\M

What a Club!

Welcome to our weird and wonderful science club: **The Lab Rats!**
Meet the Rats, check out our cool science projects, find out more about our club, visit our school, and see how we did in the Science Fair!

If you want to stay with one font color on the entire page, put your chosen color inside the <body> tag as well, like this: <body text=?>. The <body> tag can also hold the color information for both the background and the text.

<body bg color=? text=?>

3. Change the font color of the text on your page. Add the following to the <body> tag as shown.

<body bgcolor=yellow text=red>

4. Check your result.

Address | C:\Documents and Settings\Julie & Joe\My Documents\labrats.html | ⌄ → Go

What a Club!

Welcome to our weird and wonderful science club: **The Lab Rats!** Meet the Rats, check out our cool science projects, find out more about our club, visit our school, and see how we did in the Science Fair!

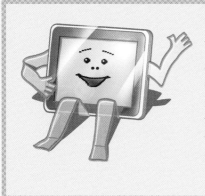

Byte Box

You may choose from one of the 216 "browser safe" colors on a color chart. Each color on the chart has a code consisting of six numbers, letters, or a combination of both. For example, the code for yellow is FFFF00. When you write the tag, you use the code instead of a color name. You can find a color chart by typing "web design color chart" into a search engine.

Add Color to Certain Words

If you want to change the color of certain words, use the following opening and closing tags. For example: <font color=?>your text</font>. Change the "?" to the color name or code you want for that text.

1. Change the word "cool" in your text from red to green by typing the tags shown on the screen on the right.

```
labrats - Notepad
File  Edit  Format  View  Help
<body bgcolor=yellow text=red>
<h2 align=center>What a Club!</h2>
<font face=Arial size=5>Welcome</font>
to our weird and wonderful science club:
<b>The Lab Rats!</b>
<br>
Meet the Rats, check out our
<font color=green>cool</font> science
projects, find out more about our club,
<a href=http://www.yourschoolwebaddress>
visit our school</a>, and see how we did in
the Science Fair!
</body>
</html>
```

2. Save your file.

3. Open, reload, or refresh your browser. Your screen should look like the one below.

Address C:\Documents and Settings\Julie & Joe\My Documents\labrats.html   Go

What a Club!

Welcome to our weird and wonderful science club: **The Lab Rats!**
Meet the Rats, check out our cool science projects, find out more about our club, **visit our school**, and see how we did in the Science Fair!

Adding Images

Images, whether they are photographs or illustrations, are attractive additions to many Web sites. Making images yourself may require expensive software, however, you can use free images called **clip art**. Check the package of software that came with your computer to see if you have a clip art program. If you search for free art on the Web, remember that most images you see on the Web belong to someone, so you cannot use them without their permission.

There are other ways to obtain images. If you have access to a digital camera, you can **download** pictures onto your computer. Most film and camera stores will develop your film and put the pictures on a Web site or CD for you. You could also scan your own pictures and drawings (or pay to have them scanned at a copy shop). Remember you don't want to put photographs of yourself or family on your Web site.

Image Formats

There are two common image file formats for the Web: GIF (Graphic Interchange Format) and JPEG (Joint Photographic Experts Group format, usually written as JPG). In general, a JPG format is better for photos and complex images because it compresses each image so that it takes less memory space when stored in your computer. The GIF format works well for simple line drawings.

If you plan to use an image that is not in one of these formats, it usually must be converted, using an image editor, such as Paintshop Pro®, or Adobe Photoshop®. (Computers often come from the supplier with image editors.)

Store your images in the same folder as your HTML file so the browser doesn't have to dig up the whole backyard looking for them!

To convert a file,

1. Open the file in an image editor.

2. Click the *File* tab on the toolbar.

3. Select *Save as* from the drop-down menu.

4. Save your file in the format you desire. End the name in either .gif or .jpg so your browser will recognize that the file is an image.

Sizing an Image

It is also possible to reduce or enlarge your image in the image editors. You can choose the perfect size for your image before you put it into your Web page. The image we are using in this book is 142 **pixels** (width) by 147 pixels (height).

Placing an Image

To place an image on your Web page, use the following tag, which is an abbreviation for *image source*: <img src=?>. Replace "?" with the name of the image file. If the Lab Rats had a photo of a science experiment they wanted to add to the Web site, they could name the image file *labrats.jpg*. They would put the image file in the same folder as the *labrats.html* file.

Try inserting an image file by typing the tag to the right in your text to show where the image might go.

```
labrats - Notepad
File   Edit   Format   View   Help
<body bgcolor=yellow text=red>
<img src=labrats.jpg><h2 align=center>What a Club!</h2>
<font face=Arial size=5>Welcome</font> to our weird and
wonderful science club:
<b>The Lab Rats!</b>
<br>
Meet the Rats, check out our
<font color=green>cool</font> science projects, find out
more about our club,
<a href=http://www.yourschoolwebaddress>visit our
school</a>, and see how we did in the Science Fair!</body>
</html>
```

The *labrats.jpg* file is just an example name. With no real file in the folder, you will just see a small blank box on the Web page in your browser.

What a Club!

Welcome to our weird and wonderful science club: The Lab Rats!
Meet the Rats, check out our cool science projects, find out more about our club, visit our school, and see how we did in the Science Fair!

Alignment, Borders, and Wrapping Text

An image usually aligns to the left just like text. However, you can move it to the right margin by using a tag like this: <img align=right src=?>.

To center an image, use this tag: <img align=center src=?>. To make this tag work, you first might have to center the paragraph of text near the image, like this.

```
<p align=center>
<img src=?>
```

1. Add to your image tag to center your image by typing the tag as shown on the screen below.

labrats - Notepad

File Edit Format View Help

```
<body bgcolor=yellow text=red>
<p align=center>
<img align=center src=labrats.jpg><h2 align=center>
What a Club!</h2><font face=Arial size=5>Welcome
</font> to our weird and wonderful science club:
<b>The Lab Rats!</b>
<br>
Meet the Rats, check out our <font color=green>cool
</font> science projects, find out more about our club,
<a href=http://www.yourschoolwebaddress>visit our
school</a>, and see how we did in the Science Fair!
</body>
</html>
```

- Microsoft Internet Explorer

vorites   Tools   Help

ts and Settings\Julie & Joe\My Documents\labrats.html

What a Club!

Welcome to our weird and wonderful science club: **The Lab Rats!**
Meet the Rats, check out our cool science projects, find out more about our club, visit our school, and see how we did in the Science Fair!

If you would like to put a border or frame around a picture, use the following tag: <img border=# src=?>. Replace "#" with a border size (which is in pixels); 0 means no border and 99 is a very thick one. Remember, that "?" should be replaced with the name of the image file. On most browsers you can make the border black by adding the tag <font color=black>, with a closing tag </font>.

2. Use the *labrats.jpg* file to include all of your image values, called **attributes**, in one tag, like the HTML code screen here.

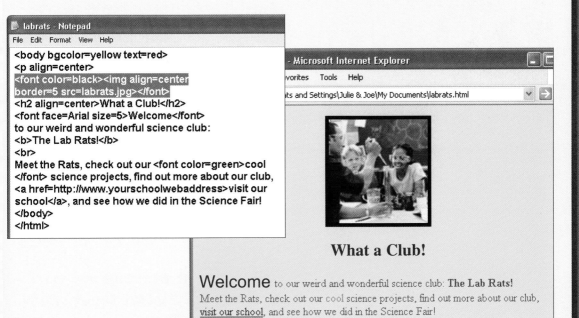

Text that surrounds a picture is called wrapping text. To have an image on the left of your Web page with text running down along the right side of the image, use the following tag before the first word of the text: <p><img align=left src=?>. To reverse this instruction, use this text: <p><img align=right src=?>.

3. Wrap some text around your image. Type the <p> tag before the first word of the text, and then place the image tag inside the text. You may have to build in breaks <br> to show how long you want each line of text.

```
labrats - Notepad
File  Edit  Format  View  Help

<body bgcolor=yellow text=red>
<p>We are the Lab Rats. We meet on
<br><font color=black><img align=right
border=5 src=labrats.jpg></font>
the first Wednesday of each month<br>
to explore the world of science.
<h2 align=center>What a Club!</h2>
<font face=Arial size=5>Welcome</font>
to our weird and wonderful science club:
<b>The Lab Rats!</b>
<br>
Meet the Rats, check out our <font color=green>cool
</font> science projects, find out more about our club,
<a href=http://www.yourschoolwebaddress>visit our
school</a>, and see how we did in the Science Fair!
</body>
</html>
```

Keep digging for more tags and more knowledge. Check out the useful sites on page 39. Keep practicing and learning, and keep having fun!

```
Meet The Lab Rats - Microsoft Internet Explorer
File  Edit  View  Favorites  Tools  Help
Address  C:\Documents and Settings\Julie & Joe\My Documents\labrats.html    Go
```

We are the Lab Rats. We meet on
the first Wednesday of each month
to explore the world of science.

What a Club!

Welcome to our weird and wonderful science club:
The Lab Rats!
Meet the Rats, check out our cool science projects, find out
more about our club, <u>visit our school</u>, and see how we did in the Science Fair!

Putting It Together

To help you see how the parts fit together, let's return to The Lab Rats and assume that they have the following:

- labrats.html (a file for the home page)
- projects.html (a file describing several science projects)
- clubinfo.html (a file about the club)
- labrats.jpg (a file with a photo of a science project)
- http://www.yourschoolwebaddress (URL address for your school)
- http://www.yourschoolwebaddress/sciencefair.html (URL address for the science fair)

Now, using this information and what you have learned so far, let's create a Web site that has a picture and **internal** and **external links**. An internal link connects files on your computer, both HTML and image files. An external link connects your Web page to another site on the World Wide Web. When you create an internal link, you only need to include the name of the file in the opening tag, as in this example: <a href=projects.html>. All files for internal links should be in the same folder as the HTML file.

Byte Box

Use breaks to keep your site from being too wide or too tall for other monitors or printers. An image or text that is too wide may have its edge chopped off when printed. You can always have a second page with more material and link it with a hot spot, the word BACK, to the first page. On the first page, use the word NEXT as a hot spot link to the second page.

1. Return to your HTML file.

2. Add the highlighted text and tags below to your file.

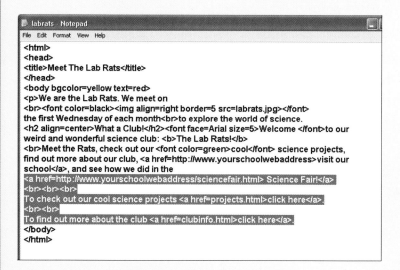

3. Save your file. Open, reload, or refresh your browser. Your screen should look like this.

Hello, World Wide Web!

Now that you've seen how to make a Web site, you can plan one of your own. Visit sites that you like and take notes about what makes them interesting and fun. Take a look at the HTML code of these sites to get some ideas on how to create the effects that you want (see p. 7). Then write the files to build it. Remember to follow the safety rules on page 5, keeping all your personal information out of the public eye. The final step in creating a site is to put it online. You'll find help in the Byte Box on this page.

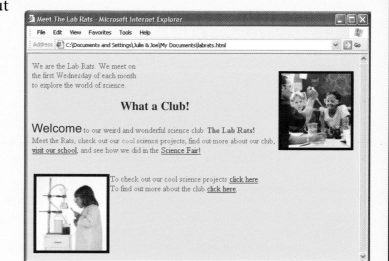

Experiment with your Web site. You can add another image by aligning the image to the left, and adding another break to your text.

Byte Box

- Your computer is connected to the Web by an **Internet Service Provider** (ISP). Your ISP may let you put your Web site files on the Web. Ask a parent or guardian to contact your ISP for details and instructions.
- You can also sign up with a free Web page provider service. A teacher, parent, or guardian can help you set up an account so you can get your own Web address. Instructions can be found at the service provider's site.

Glossary

align	line up certain parts of a page
attributes	qualities or components of your Web site, such as the way the text is aligned, its size, and color, that are determined by tag coding
browser	computer software that translates HTML code into a text-based language
clip art	existing images, including photos and illustrations, that can be added to your Web page
download	to transfer a file from the Web or another computer to your computer
external link	a connection highlighted on a Web site that links to another Web address
font	a set of letters and numbers in a particular design or style used to create text on your Web page
HTML (HyperText Markup Language)	a programming language used to build Web sites
internal link	a connection highlighted on a Web site that links to another page on the same site
Internet	a large computer network, made up of thousands of smaller networks
Internet Service Provider (ISP)	a company that provides access to the Internet

network	a system of connected computers
pixels	tiny colored dots that make up an image on a computer screen
search engine	a computer program or Web site used to find information on the Internet
tags	special signal codes that tell the browser what action to take
URL (Universal Resource Locator)	a World Wide Web address
World Wide Web	a group of Internet sites that are interconnected, providing access to information, images, and sounds

Useful Web Sites

For HTML help, including color charts, HTML reference sheets, and other tools, see these sites:
http://www.htmlhelp.com
http://www.goodellgroup.com/tutorial
http://www.lissaexplains.com
http://www.hotwired.lycos.com/webmonkey/kids

For clip art, try these:
http://www.clip-art.com
http://www.awesomeclipartforkids.com
http://www.kidsdomain.com/clip

Index